Published by Angelis Publications
ISBN: 978-0-9956949-9-6
Cover Design Angie J Anderson

Wherever you go, go with all your heart. Confucius. Wherever you go, go with all your heart. Confucius. Wherever you go, go with all your heart. Confucius. Wherever you go, go with all your heart. Confucius.

Welcome!

Date / Name / From ...	Comments

Would you be willing to let us share your testimonial? If so, please scribble your initials after your comments. Thank you!

Date / Name / From ...	Comments

Would you be willing to let us share your testimonial? If so, please scribble your initials after your comments. Thank you!

Date / Name / From ...	Comments

Would you be willing to let us share your testimonial? If so, please scribble your initials after your comments. Thank you!

Date / Name / From ... | Comments

Would you be willing to let us share your testimonial? If so, please scribble your initials after your comments. Thank you!

Date / Name / From ...	Comments

Would you be willing to let us share your testimonial? If so, please scribble your initials after your comments. Thank you!

Date / Name / From ...	Comments

Would you be willing to let us share your testimonial? If so, please scribble your initials after your comments. Thank you!

Date / Name / From ...	Comments

Would you be willing to let us share your testimonial? If so, please scribble your initials after your comments. Thank you!

Date / Name / From ...	Comments

Would you be willing to let us share your testimonial? If so, please scribble your initials after your comments. Thank you!

Date / Name / From ... | Comments

Would you be willing to let us share your testimonial? If so, please scribble your initials after your comments. Thank you!

Date / Name / From ...	Comments

Would you be willing to let us share your testimonial? If so, please scribble your initials after your comments. Thank you!

Date / Name / From ...	Comments

Would you be willing to let us share your testimonial? If so, please scribble your initials after your comments. Thank you!

Date / Name / From ...	Comments

Would you be willing to let us share your testimonial? If so, please scribble your initials after your comments. Thank you!

Date / Name / From ...	Comments

Would you be willing to let us share your testimonial? If so, please scribble your initials after your comments. Thank you!

Date / Name / From ... | Comments

Would you be willing to let us share your testimonial? If so, please scribble your initials after your comments. Thank you!

Date / Name / From ...	Comments

Would you be willing to let us share your testimonial? If so, please scribble your initials after your comments. Thank you!

Date / Name / From ...	Comments

Would you be willing to let us share your testimonial? If so, please scribble your initials after your comments. Thank you!

Date / Name / From ...	Comments

Would you be willing to let us share your testimonial? If so, please scribble your initials after your comments. Thank you!

Date / Name / From ... | Comments

Would you be willing to let us share your testimonial? If so, please scribble your initials after your comments. Thank you!

Date / Name / From ...	Comments

Would you be willing to let us share your testimonial? If so, please scribble your initials after your comments. Thank you!

Date / Name / From ...	Comments

Would you be willing to let us share your testimonial? If so, please scribble your initials after your comments. Thank you!

Date / Name / From ...	Comments

Would you be willing to let us share your testimonial? If so, please scribble your initials after your comments. Thank you!

Date / Name / From ...	Comments

Would you be willing to let us share your testimonial? If so, please scribble your initials after your comments. Thank you!

Date / Name / From ...	Comments

Would you be willing to let us share your testimonial? If so, please scribble your initials after your comments. Thank you!

Date / Name / From ...	Comments

Would you be willing to let us share your testimonial? If so, please scribble your initials after your comments. Thank you!

Date / Name / From ...	Comments

Would you be willing to let us share your testimonial? If so, please scribble your initials after your comments. Thank you!

Date / Name / From ...	Comments

Would you be willing to let us share your testimonial? If so, please scribble your initials after your comments. Thank you!

Date / Name / From ...	Comments

Would you be willing to let us share your testimonial? If so, please scribble your initials after your comments. Thank you!

Date / Name / From ...	Comments

Would you be willing to let us share your testimonial? If so, please scribble your initials after your comments. Thank you!

Date / Name / From ...	Comments

Would you be willing to let us share your testimonial? If so, please scribble your initials after your comments. Thank you!

Date / Name / From ...	Comments

Would you be willing to let us share your testimonial? If so, please scribble your initials after your comments. Thank you!

Date / Name / From ...	Comments

Would you be willing to let us share your testimonial? If so, please scribble your initials after your comments. Thank you!

Date / Name / From ...	Comments

Would you be willing to let us share your testimonial? If so, please scribble your initials after your comments. Thank you!

Date / Name / From ...	Comments

Would you be willing to let us share your testimonial? If so, please scribble your initials after your comments. Thank you!

Date / Name / From ...	Comments

Would you be willing to let us share your testimonial? If so, please scribble your initials after your comments. Thank you!

Date / Name / From ...	Comments

Would you be willing to let us share your testimonial? If so, please scribble your initials after your comments. Thank you!

Date / Name / From ...	Comments

Would you be willing to let us share your testimonial? If so, please scribble your initials after your comments. Thank you!

Date / Name / From ...	Comments

Would you be willing to let us share your testimonial? If so, please scribble your initials after your comments. Thank you!

Date / Name / From ...	Comments

Would you be willing to let us share your testimonial? If so, please scribble your initials after your comments. Thank you!

Date / Name / From ...	Comments

Would you be willing to let us share your testimonial? If so, please scribble your initials after your comments. Thank you!

Date / Name / From ...	Comments

Would you be willing to let us share your testimonial? If so, please scribble your initials after your comments. Thank you!

Date / Name / From ... | Comments

Would you be willing to let us share your testimonial? If so, please scribble your initials after your comments. Thank you!

Date / Name / From ...	Comments

Would you be willing to let us share your testimonial? If so, please scribble your initials after your comments. Thank you!

Date / Name / From ...	Comments

Would you be willing to let us share your testimonial? If so, please scribble your initials after your comments. Thank you!

Date / Name / From ...	Comments

Would you be willing to let us share your testimonial? If so, please scribble your initials after your comments. Thank you!

Date / Name / From ...	Comments

Would you be willing to let us share your testimonial? If so, please scribble your initials after your comments. Thank you!

Date / Name / From ... | Comments

Would you be willing to let us share your testimonial? If so, please scribble your initials after your comments. Thank you!

Date / Name / From ...	Comments

Would you be willing to let us share your testimonial? If so, please scribble your initials after your comments. Thank you!

Date / Name / From ...	Comments

Would you be willing to let us share your testimonial? If so, please scribble your initials after your comments. Thank you!

Date / Name / From ...	Comments

Would you be willing to let us share your testimonial? If so, please scribble your initials after your comments. Thank you!

Date / Name / From ...	Comments

Would you be willing to let us share your testimonial? If so, please scribble your initials after your comments. Thank you!

Date / Name / From ...	Comments

Would you be willing to let us share your testimonial? If so, please scribble your initials after your comments. Thank you!

Date / Name / From ...	Comments

Would you be willing to let us share your testimonial? If so, please scribble your initials after your comments. Thank you!

Date / Name / From ...	Comments

Would you be willing to let us share your testimonial? If so, please scribble your initials after your comments. Thank you!

Date / Name / From ...	Comments

Would you be willing to let us share your testimonial? If so, please scribble your initials after your comments. Thank you!

Date / Name / From ...	Comments

Would you be willing to let us share your testimonial? If so, please scribble your initials after your comments. Thank you!

Date / Name / From ...	Comments

Would you be willing to let us share your testimonial? If so, please scribble your initials after your comments. Thank you!

Date / Name / From ...	Comments

Would you be willing to let us share your testimonial? If so, please scribble your initials after your comments. Thank you!

Date / Name / From ...	Comments

Would you be willing to let us share your testimonial? If so, please scribble your initials after your comments. Thank you!

Date / Name / From ...	Comments

Would you be willing to let us share your testimonial? If so, please scribble your initials after your comments. Thank you!

Date / Name / From ... | Comments

Would you be willing to let us share your testimonial? If so, please scribble your initials after your comments. Thank you!

Date / Name / From ...	Comments

Would you be willing to let us share your testimonial? If so, please scribble your initials after your comments. Thank you!

Date / Name / From ...	Comments

Would you be willing to let us share your testimonial? If so, please scribble your initials after your comments. Thank you!

Date / Name / From ...	Comments

Would you be willing to let us share your testimonial? If so, please scribble your initials after your comments. Thank you!

Date / Name / From ...

Comments

Would you be willing to let us share your testimonial? If so, please scribble your initials after your comments. Thank you!

Date / Name / From ...	Comments

Would you be willing to let us share your testimonial? If so, please scribble your initials after your comments. Thank you!

Date / Name / From ...	Comments

Would you be willing to let us share your testimonial? If so, please scribble your initials after your comments. Thank you!

Date / Name / From ...	Comments

Would you be willing to let us share your testimonial? If so, please scribble your initials after your comments. Thank you!

Date / Name / From ...	Comments

Would you be willing to let us share your testimonial? If so, please scribble your initials after your comments. Thank you!

Date / Name / From ...	Comments

Would you be willing to let us share your testimonial? If so, please scribble your initials after your comments. Thank you!

Date / Name / From ...	Comments

Would you be willing to let us share your testimonial? If so, please scribble your initials after your comments. Thank you!

Date / Name / From ...	Comments

Would you be willing to let us share your testimonial? If so, please scribble your initials after your comments. Thank you!

Date / Name / From ...	Comments

Would you be willing to let us share your testimonial? If so, please scribble your initials after your comments. Thank you!

Date / Name / From ...	Comments

Would you be willing to let us share your testimonial? If so, please scribble your initials after your comments. Thank you!

Date / Name / From ...	Comments

Would you be willing to let us share your testimonial? If so, please scribble your initials after your comments. Thank you!

Date / Name / From ...	Comments

Would you be willing to let us share your testimonial? If so, please scribble your initials after your comments. Thank you!

Date / Name / From ...	Comments

Would you be willing to let us share your testimonial? If so, please scribble your initials after your comments. Thank you!

Date / Name / From ...	Comments

Would you be willing to let us share your testimonial? If so, please scribble your initials after your comments. Thank you!

Date / Name / From ...	Comments

Would you be willing to let us share your testimonial? If so, please scribble your initials after your comments. Thank you!

Date / Name / From ...	Comments

Would you be willing to let us share your testimonial? If so, please scribble your initials after your comments. Thank you!

Date / Name / From ...	Comments

Would you be willing to let us share your testimonial? If so, please scribble your initials after your comments. Thank you!

Date / Name / From ...	Comments

Would you be willing to let us share your testimonial? If so, please scribble your initials after your comments. Thank you!

Date / Name / From ...	Comments

Would you be willing to let us share your testimonial? If so, please scribble your initials after your comments. Thank you!

Date / Name / From ...	Comments

Would you be willing to let us share your testimonial? If so, please scribble your initials after your comments. Thank you!

Date / Name / From ...	Comments

Would you be willing to let us share your testimonial? If so, please scribble your initials after your comments. Thank you!

Date / Name / From ...	Comments

Would you be willing to let us share your testimonial? If so, please scribble your initials after your comments. Thank you!

Date / Name / From ... | Comments

Would you be willing to let us share your testimonial? If so, please scribble your initials after your comments. Thank you!

Date / Name / From ...	Comments

Would you be willing to let us share your testimonial? If so, please scribble your initials after your comments. Thank you!

Date / Name / From ...	Comments

Would you be willing to let us share your testimonial? If so, please scribble your initials after your comments. Thank you!

Date / Name / From ...	Comments

Would you be willing to let us share your testimonial? If so, please scribble your initials after your comments. Thank you!

Date / Name / From ...	Comments

Would you be willing to let us share your testimonial? If so, please scribble your initials after your comments. Thank you!

Date / Name / From ...	Comments

Would you be willing to let us share your testimonial? If so, please scribble your initials after your comments. Thank you!

Date / Name / From ...	Comments

Would you be willing to let us share your testimonial? If so, please scribble your initials after your comments. Thank you!

Date / Name / From ...	Comments

Would you be willing to let us share your testimonial? If so, please scribble your initials after your comments. Thank you!

Date / Name / From ...	Comments

Would you be willing to let us share your testimonial? If so, please scribble your initials after your comments. Thank you!

Date / Name / From ...	Comments

Would you be willing to let us share your testimonial? If so, please scribble your initials after your comments. Thank you!

Date / Name / From ... | Comments

Would you be willing to let us share your testimonial? If so, please scribble your initials after your comments. Thank you!

www.ingramcontent.com/pod-product-compliance
Lightning Source LLC
Chambersburg PA
CBHW081126300726
48982CB00005B/864

* 9 7 8 0 9 9 5 6 9 4 9 9 6 *